INFINITE
MIND POWER

INFINITE MIND POWER

JOSEPH MURPHY
*The Power of Your
Subconscious Mind*

CHARLES FILLMORE
Atom-Smashing Power of Mind

ROBERT COLLIER
The Secret of the Ages

ABRIDGED AND INTRODUCED BY
MITCH HOROWITZ

MEDIA

Published by Gildan Media LLC
aka G&D Media.
www.GandDmedia.com

The Power of Your Subconscious Mind was originally published in 1963
Atom-Smashing Power of Mind was originally published in 1949
The Secret of the Ages was originally published in 1925 as *The Book of Life*. It appeared under its current title in 1926, and was revised by the author in 1948.
G&D Media Condensed Classics editions published 2019
Abridgement and Introduction copyright © 2019 by Mitch Horowitz

FIRST EDITION: 2019

Cover design by David Rheinhardt of Pyrographx

Interior design by Meghan Day Healey of Story Horse, LLC.

ISBN: 978-1-7225-0221-8

Contents

Introduction

Of Spririt and Science
By Mitch Horowitz

Each of the three classics condensed in this collection shares two things in common. First, these are some of the most popular and clearly written modern works on the causative powers of the mind. And second, each writer sees his mystical insights as coalescing perfectly with, and supported by, the revolutions in modern science.

The Power of Your Subconscious Mind by Joseph Murphy, *Atom-Smashing Power of Mind* by Charles Fillmore, and *The Secret of the Ages* by Robert Collier were written at hopeful junctures in the twentieth-century when spiritual writers and social thinkers believed that the yearning for human progress and betterment could converge into a holistic philosophy, which would improve and benefit the lives of all people. Some of us still hold to that somewhat battered ideal today. You may find this hope swelling up anew within you as you experience the practical ideas in these earnestly written and deeply actionable books of popular philosophy and spiritual-psychology.

Written in 1963, *The Power of Your Subconscious Mind* sees the interior mind as harboring extraordinary properties of Higher Intelligence, which outpicture into the events of our lives.

Atom-Smashing Power of Mind, published in 1949 just after the dawn of the atomic age, argues that thought is the one-and-only power in the universe, and that it is synonymous with the same awesome energy unleashed by the splitting of the atom.

Finally, *The Secret of the Ages*, written in 1926, sees mental causation as the hidden power behind every event depicted in Scripture and myth, and in humanity's new understandings of evolution, cosmic order, and the wonders of natural science.

Each of these abridgments is filled with practical ideas on how to harness the higher psychology that the authors' perceive as the human birthright. And each book is epic in scale, finding within the insights of science confirmation of humanity's highest strivings and assessments of itself.

THE POWER
OF YOUR
SUBCONSCIOUS
MIND

THE POWER
OF YOUR
SUBCONSCIOUS
MIND

by Joseph Murphy

The Original Classic

Abridged and Introduced
by Mitch Horowitz

THE CONDENSED 📖 CLASSICS LIBRARY™

Contents

The Power of Thought

This may be one of the most personally important books you ever encounter. I say that not because I agree with every one of its premises or ideas. But, rather, because author and New Thought minister Joseph Murphy identifies and expands upon one immensely important and undervalued principle: *What you think dramatically affects your quality of life.*

This idea has been restated from antiquity to the present. John Milton put it this way in *Paradise Lost*: "The mind is its own place, and in it self can make a Heav'n of Hell, a Hell of Heav'n."

Murphy presents this principle as an absolute. He argues that thought governs health, finances, relationships, and all facets of life. I am personally unconvinced that *every* element of existence yields to thought alone. But within the folds of this idea—that mind is the master builder—can be found great truths. They are yours to discover, test, and benefit from. All that is required is to change how you think.

Murphy's philosophy is profoundly simple—but it is not for the weak or myopic. If you take seriously what you find in this book—and I urge you to—you will discover that redirecting your thoughts toward resiliency and constructiveness requires a lifetime of effort. But it is a task worthy of every motivated, mature person.

You will also learn that your emotions must be brought into play for any real self-change to occur. Emotion is more powerful than thought—never confuse or conflate the two. The mind says, "be satisfied with your portion"—emotion shouts, "I want more!" The mind says, "be calm"—emotion wants to run away. The mind says, "I'm happy for my neighbor"—emotion feels envy. Murphy supplies exercises to help align your emotions and thoughts in pursuit of a personal goal.

Murphy's message that *new thought means new life* has touched countless people since this book first appeared in 1963. This is not because Murphy's outlook is cloying or wishful; but because it is essentially true. We *all* feel that we should be practicing more dignified, generous, and self-respecting patterns of thought, tones of speech, and person-to-person relations. We harbor the conviction that we are *not* leading the lives we should be—that our abilities are underdeveloped, our decisions too hesitant and timorous, and our attitudes too selfish. Almost all of us sense the potential of a larger existence within us. This is a near-universal instinct.

The Power of Your Subconscious Mind is an instruction manual toward seeking that greater scale of life. Pay close attention to the book's principles, methods, and exercises. And, above all, *use them*.

It may be the most important step you ever take.

—Mitch Horowitz

Chapter One

The Treasure House
Within You

What, in your opinion, is the master secret of the ages? Atomic power? Thermonuclear energy? Interplanetary travel? No—not any of these. What, then, is the master secret? Where can one find it, and how can it be contacted and brought into action? The answer is extraordinarily simple. The secret is the marvelous, miracle-working power of your own subconscious mind.

You can bring into your life more ability, more health, more wealth, and more happiness by learning to contact and release the hidden forces of your subconscious.

As you follow the simple techniques in this book, you can gain the necessary knowledge and understanding to unlock your subconscious depths. Within them are infinite wisdom, infinite power, and infinite supply. Begin now to recognize these potentialities of your deeper mind, and they will take form in the world without.

The infinite intelligence within your subconscious can reveal to you everything you need to know at every moment, provided you are open-minded and receptive. You can receive new thoughts and ideas enabling you to bring forth new inventions, make new discoveries, or write plays and books. You can attract the ideal companion. You can acquire resources and wealth. You can move forward in abundance, security, joy, and dominion.

It is your *right* to discover this inner world of thought. Its miracle-working powers and eternal laws of life existed before you were born, before any religion or church appeared, and before the world itself came into being. It is with these thoughts that I urge you in the following chapters to lay hold of this wonderful, magical, transforming power that is your subconscious mind.

CHAPTER TWO

How Your Mind Works

There are two levels of mind, conscious and subconscious. You think with your rational, conscious mind—and whatever you habitually think seeps down into your subconscious mind, which creates according to the nature of your thoughts.

Once the subconscious mind accepts an idea, it begins to execute it. Your subconscious does not engage in *proving* whether your thoughts are good or bad, but responds according to the *nature* of your thoughts or suggestions. If you consciously assume something is true, even though it may be false, your subconscious will accept it and proceed to bring about results that must necessarily follow.

Your conscious mind is the "watchman at the gate." Its chief function is to protect your subconscious from false impressions. You now know one of the basic laws of mind: Your subconscious is amenable to *suggestion*.

From infancy on, many of us have been given negative suggestions. Not knowing how to thwart them, we unconsciously accepted them. Here are some of the negative suggestions: "You can't." "You'll never amount to anything." "You'll fail." "You haven't got a chance." "It's no use." "It's not what you know, but who you know." "You're too old now." And so on.

If you look back, you can easily recall how parents, friends, relatives, teachers, and associates contributed to a campaign of negative suggestions. Study the things said to you, and you will discover that much of it was said to control you or instill fear in you. Check regularly on the negative suggestions that people make to you today. You do not have to be influenced by destructive suggestion.

Never say: "I can't." Overcome fear of failure by substituting the following statement: *I can do all things through the power of my subconscious mind.*

Never allow others to think for you. Choose your own thoughts, and make your own decisions. Always remember that *you have the capacity to choose*. Choose life! Choose love! Choose health! Choose happiness! Whatever your conscious mind assumes and believes, your subconscious mind accepts and brings to pass.

CHAPTER THREE

The Miracle-Working Power of Your Subconscious Mind

The power of your subconscious mind is enormous. It inspires you, guides you, and reveals to you names, facts, and scenes from the storehouse of memory.

Your subconscious mind never sleeps or rests. You can discover its miracle-working power by plainly stating to your subconscious prior to sleep that you wish to accomplish a certain thing. You will be delighted to find that forces within you will be released, leading to the desired answer or result.

William James, the father of American psychology, said that the power to move the world resides within your subconscious mind. Your subconscious is at one with infinite intelligence and boundless wisdom. It is fed by hidden springs. The law of life operates through it. Whatever you impress upon your subconscious, it will move heaven and earth to bring it to pass. You must, therefore, impress it with right ideas and constructive thoughts.

What is your idea or feeling about yourself right now? Every part of your being expresses that idea. Your body, vitality, finances, friends, and social status are a perfect reflection of the idea you have of yourself. What is impressed in your subconscious mind is expressed in all phases of your life.

Worry, anxiety, and fear can interfere with the normal rhythm of your heart, lungs, and other organs. Feed your subconscious mind with thoughts of harmony, health, and peace, and all the functions of your body will become normal again.

Feel the thrill of accomplishment, imagine the happy ending or solution to your problem, and what you imagine and feel will be accepted by your subconscious mind and brought to pass. The life principle will flow through you rhythmically and harmoniously as you consciously affirm: *I believe that the subconscious power that gave me this desire is now fulfilling it through me.*

Your subconscious mind can and will accomplish as much as you allow it to.

CHAPTER FOUR

Prayer and Your Subconscious Mind

I n building the Golden Gate Bridge, the chief engineer understood mathematical principles, stresses, and strains. Secondly, he had a picture of the ideal bridge across the bay. The third step was his application of tried and proven methods, which were implemented until the bridge took form. Likewise, there exist techniques and methods by which your prayers are actualized.

Prayer is the formulation of an idea concerning something you wish to accomplish. Your desire *is* your prayer. It comes out of your deepest needs and it reveals what you want in life. *Blessed are they that hunger and thirst after righteousness: for they shall be filled.* That is really prayer: life's hunger and thirst for peace, harmony, health, joy, and other blessings.

We will now explore the "passing over" technique for impregnating the subconscious mind with your desire. This involves inducing the subconscious to *take over* your prayer request as handed it by the conscious mind. This *passing over* is best accomplished in a reverie-like state. Know that within your deeper mind exist infinite intelligence and infinite power. Just calmly think over what you want; and see it coming into fuller fruition from this moment forward.

Your prayer—*your mental act*—must be accepted as an image in your mind before the power of your subconscious will play upon it and make it operative. You must reach a point of *acceptance* in your mind, an unqualified and undisputed state of agreement.

This contemplation should be accompanied by a feeling of joy and restfulness in foreseeing the accomplishment of your desire. The basis for the art and science of true prayer is your knowledge and complete confidence that the movement of your conscious mind will gain a definite response from your subconscious mind.

The easiest and most obvious way to formulate an idea is to visualize it, to see it in your mind's eye as vividly as if it were alive. You can see with the naked eye only what already exists in the external world; in a similar way, that which you can visualize in your mind's eye *already exists* in the infinite realms of thought. Any picture that you have in your mind is *the substance of things hoped for and the evidence of things not seen.* What you form in your imagination is as real as any part of your body.

Your ideas and thoughts are *real*—and will one day appear in the objective world if you remain faithful to your mental image.

CHAPTER FIVE

How to Get the Results You Want

The principle reasons for failure when trying to tap your subconscious are: 1) lack of confidence, and 2) too much effort.

Many people block answers to their prayers by failing to fully comprehend the nature of their subconscious. When you know how your mind functions, you gain a measure of *confidence*. You must remember that whenever your subconscious accepts an idea, it immediately begins to execute it. It uses all its mighty resources to that end, and mobilizes all the mental and spiritual faculties of your deeper mind. This law is true for good ideas or bad. Consequently, if you use it negatively, it brings trouble, failure, and confusion. When you use it constructively, it brings guidance, freedom, and peace.

The right answer is inevitable when your thoughts are constructive and loving. The only thing you have to do to overcome failure is to get your subconscious to accept your idea or request by *feeling its reality now*, and the law of your mind will do the rest. Turn over the request with faith and confidence, and your subconscious will take over and see it through.

You will always fail to get results by trying to use *mental coercion*—your subconscious does not respond to coercion; it responds to your faith or conscious-mind acceptance. Relaxation is the key. *Easy does it*. Do not be concerned with details and means, but rest in the assured end.

Feeling is the touchstone of all subconscious demonstration. Your new idea must be *felt subjectively*, not in the future but in a finished state, as coming about now. Get the *feel* of the happy solution to your problem. Remember how you felt in the past when you solved a major problem or recovered from a serious illness. Live in this feeling, and your subconscious depths will bring it to pass.

CHAPTER SIX

How to Use Your Subconscious Mind for Wealth

Wealth is a subconscious conviction on the part of the individual. You will not become a millionaire by saying, "I am a millionaire, I am a millionaire." Rather, you will *grow into a wealth consciousness* by building into your mentality the idea of wealth and abundance.

Perhaps you are saying to yourself now, "I need wealth and success." Follow these steps: Repeat for about five minutes to yourself three or four times a day, "Wealth—Success." These words have tremendous power. They represent the inner power of the subconscious. Anchor your mind on this substantial power within you; then corresponding conditions and circumstances will be manifested in your life.

Again, you are not merely saying, "I am wealthy." You are dwelling on real powers within you. There is no conflict in the mind when you say, "Wealth." Furthermore, the *feeling* of wealth will well up within you as you dwell on the idea of wealth.

I have talked to many people during the past thirty-five years whose usual complaint is: "I have said for weeks and months, 'I am wealthy, I am prosperous,' and nothing has happened." I discovered that when they said, "I am prosperous, I am wealthy," they felt within that they were lying to themselves. One man told me, "I have affirmed that I am prosperous until I am tired. Things are now worse. I knew when I made that statement that it was obviously not true." His statements were rejected by the conscious mind, and the very opposite of what he outwardly affirmed was made manifest.

Your affirmation succeeds best when it is specific and when it does not produce a mental conflict or argument; hence, the statements made by this man made matters worse because they suggested his lack. Your subconscious mind accepts what you really feel to be true, not just idle words or statements.

Here is the ideal way to overcome this conflict. Make this statement frequently, particularly prior to sleep: *By day and by night I am being prospered in all of my interests.* This affirmation will not arouse any argument because it does not contradict your subconscious mind's impression of financial lack.

Many people tell themselves, "I deserve a higher salary." I believe that most people are, in fact, underpaid. One reason why many people do not have more money is that they are silently or openly condemning it. They call money "filthy lucre" or say "love of money is the root of all evil." Another reason they do not prosper is that they have a sneaky subconscious feeling that there is some virtue in poverty. This subconscious pattern may be due to early childhood training, superstition, or a mistaken interpretation of Scripture

Cleanse your mind of all conflicting beliefs about money. Do not regard money as evil or filthy. If you do, you cause it to take wings and fly away from you. You lose what you condemn.

At the same time, do not make a god of money. It is only a symbol. Remember that the real riches are in your mind. You are here to lead a balanced life—and that includes acquiring all the money you need.

There is one emotion that causes lack of wealth in the lives of many. Most people learn this the hard way. It is envy. To entertain envious thoughts is devastating; it places you in a negative position in which wealth flows *from* you rather than *to* you. If you are ever annoyed or irritated by the prosperity of another, claim immediately that you truly wish him greater wealth in every possible way. This will neutralize your negative thoughts, and cause an ever-greater measure of wealth to flow to you.

CHAPTER SEVEN

Your Subconscious Mind as a Partner in Career Success

Let us discuss three steps to success. The first step is to discover the thing you love to do, and then do it. Success is in loving your work.

Some may say, "How can I put the first step into operation? I do not know what I should do." In such a case, pray for guidance as follows: *The infinite intelligence of my subconscious mind reveals to me my true place in life.* Repeat this prayer quietly, positively, and lovingly to your deeper mind. As you persist with faith and confidence, the answer will come to you as a feeling, a hunch, or a tendency in a certain direction. It will come to you clearly and in peace, as an inner awareness.

The second step to success is to specialize in some particular branch of work, and to know more about it than anyone else. For example, if a young man chooses chemistry as his profession, he should concentrate on one of the many branches in that field. He should give all of his time and attention to his chosen specialty. He should become sufficiently enthusiastic to know all there is about it; if possible, he should know more than anyone else.

The third step is the most important. You must be certain that the thing you want to do does not build your success only. *Your desire must not be selfish; it must benefit humanity.* The path of a complete circuit must be formed. In other words, your idea must go forth with the purpose of blessing or serving the world. It will then come back to you pressed down, shaken together, and running over. If it is to benefit you alone, the circle or circuit is not formed.

A successful person loves his work and expresses himself fully. True success is contingent upon a higher ideal than mere accumulation of riches. The person of success is one who possesses great psychological and spiritual understanding, and whose work benefits others.

Chapter Eight

The Inventiveness of Your Subconscious Mind

Nikola Tesla was a brilliant electrical scientist who brought forth amazing inventions in the late-nineteenth and early twentieth centuries. When an idea for a new invention entered Tesla's mind, he would build it up in his imagination, knowing that his subconscious would construct and reveal to his conscious mind all the parts needed for its manufacture. Through quietly contemplating every possible improvement, he spent no time in correcting defects, and was able to give technicians perfect plans for the product.

"Invariably," he said, "my device works as I imagined it should. In twenty years there has not been a single exception."

When you have what you term "a difficult decision" to make, or when you fail to see the solution to a problem, begin at once to think constructively about it. If you are fearful and worried, you are not really think-ing. True thinking is free from fear.

Here is a simple technique to receive inner guid-ance on any subject: Quiet the mind and still the body. Go to a quiet place where you won't be disturbed— preferably lying on a bed, sofa, or in a recliner. Mobi-lize your attention; focus your thoughts on the solution to the problem. Try to solve it with your conscious mind. Think how happy you would be with the perfect solution. Sense the feeling you would have if the right answer were yours now. Let your mind play with this mood in a relaxed way; then drop off to sleep. When you awaken, and do not have the answer, get busy about something else. When you are preoccupied with some-thing else, the answer will probably come into your mind like toast pops from out of a toaster.

The secret of guidance or right action is to mentally devote yourself to the right answer, until you find its re-sponse in you. The response is a feeling, an inner aware-ness, and an overpowering hunch whereby *you know that you know*. In such cases, you have used the infinite power of your subconscious to the point where *it begins to use you*. You cannot fail or make a false step while operating under the subconscious wisdom within you.

CHAPTER NINE

Your Subconscious Mind and Marital Problems

R ecently a young couple, married for only a few
months, was seeking a divorce. I discovered
that the young man had a constant fear that
his wife would leave him. He expected rejection, and he
believed that she would be unfaithful. These thoughts
haunted him and became an obsession. His mental
attitude was one of separation and suspicion. His own
feeling of loss and separation operated through the rela-
tionship. This brought about a condition in accordance
with the mental pattern behind it.

His wife left home and asked for a divorce, which is
what he feared and believed would happen.

Divorce occurs first in the mind; the legal pro-
ceedings follow. These two young people were full of
resentment, fear, suspicion, and anger. These attitudes

weaken and debilitate the whole being. The couple began to realize what they had been doing with their minds. These two people returned together at my suggestion and experimented with *prayer therapy,* a method we will learn.

Each one practiced radiating to the other love, peace, harmony, health, and good will. They alternated in reading the Psalms every night. Their marriage began growing more beautiful every day.

Now, divorce is an individual problem. It cannot be generalized. In some cases, no marriage should have occurred to begin with. In other cases, divorce is not the solution. Divorce may be right for one person and wrong for another. A divorced woman may be far more sincere and noble than many of her married sisters, who are perhaps living a lie.

For couples that wish to *stay together* the solution is to *pray together*. Here is a three-step program in prayer therapy.

FIRST

Never carry over from one day to another accumulated irritations arising from little disappointments. Forgive each other for any sharpness before you retire at night. The moment you awaken, claim infinite intelligence is guiding you in all ways. Send out thoughts of peace, harmony, and love to your partner, to all family members, and to the entire world.

SECOND
Say grace at breakfast. Give thanks for the wonderful food, for your abundance, and for all your blessings. Make sure that no problems, worries, or arguments enter into the table conversation; the same applies at dinnertime. Say to your partner, "I appreciate all you are doing, and I radiate love and good will to you all day long."

THIRD
Spouses should alternate in praying each night. Do not take your marriage partner for granted. Show your appreciation and love. Think appreciation and good will, rather than condemnation, criticism, and nagging. Before going to sleep read the 23rd, 27th, and 91st Psalms; the 11th chapter of Hebrews; the 13th chapter of I Corinthians; and other great texts of the Bible.

As you practice these steps, your marriage will grow more blessed through the years.

CHAPTER TEN

Your Subconscious Mind and Happiness

There is a phrase in the Bible: *Choose ye this day whom ye will serve.*

You have the freedom to *choose happiness.* This may seem extraordinarily simple—and it is. Perhaps this is why so many people stumble over the way to happiness; they do not see the simplicity of the key to happiness. The great things of life are simple, dynamic, and creative.

St. Paul reveals how you can think your way into a life of dynamic power and happiness in these words: *Finally, brethren, whatsoever things are true, whatsoever things are honest, whatsoever things are just, whatsoever things are pure, whatsoever things are lovely, whatsoever things are of good report; if there be any virtue, and if there be any praise, think on these things.* (Philippians 4:8)

There is one very important point about being happy. You must sincerely *desire* to be happy. Some people have been depressed, dejected, and unhappy for so long that when they are suddenly made happy by some joyous news they actually feel uncomfortable. They have become so accustomed to the old mental patterns that they do not feel at home being happy. They long for the familiar depressed state.

Begin now to choose happiness. Here is how: When you open your eyes in the morning, say to yourself: *Divine order takes charge of my life today and every day. All things work together for good for me today. This is a new and wonderful day for me. There will never be another day like this one. I am divinely guided all day long, and whatever I do will prosper. Divine love surrounds me, enfolds me, and enwraps me, and I go forth in peace. Whenever my attention wanders away from what is good and constructive, I will immediately bring it back to the contemplation of that which is lovely and of good report. I am a spiritual and mental magnet attracting to myself all things that bless and prosper me. I am going to be a wonderful success in all my undertakings today. I am definitely going to be happy all day long.*

Start each day in this manner; you will then be choosing happiness.

CHAPTER ELEVEN

Your Subconscious Mind and Harmonious Relationships

Matthew 7:12 says, *All things whatsoever ye would that men should do unto you, do ye even so to them.*

This passage has outer and inner meanings. We are interested in its inner meaning, which is: As you would that men should *think* about you, think about them. As you would that men should *feel* about you, feel about them. As you would want men to *act* toward you, act toward them.

For example, you may be polite and courteous to someone in your office, but inside you are critical and resentful. Such negative thoughts are highly destructive to you. You are actually taking mental poisons, which rob you of enthusiasm, strength, guidance, and good will. These negative thoughts and emotions sink into your subconscious, and cause you all kinds of difficulties and maladies.

Matthew 7:1-2 says, *Judge not, that ye not be judged. For with what judgment ye judge, ye shall be judged; and with what measure ye shall mete, it shall be measured to you again.*

The study and application of these verses, and their inner truth, provides the key to harmonious relations. To judge is to think, to reach a mental verdict or conclusion in your mind. Your thoughts are creative, therefore, you actually create in your own experience what you think and feel about another person. It is also true that the suggestion you give to another, you give to yourself.

Now, there *are* difficult people in the world who are twisted and distorted mentally. They are malconditioned. Many are mental delinquents, argumentative, uncooperative, cantankerous, and cynical. They are sick psychologically. Many people have deformed and distorted minds, probably warped during childhood. Many have congenital deformities. You would not condemn a person who had tuberculosis, nor should you condemn someone who is mentally ill. You should have compassion and understanding. *To understand all is to forgive all.*

At the same time, do not permit people to take advantage of you and gain their point by temper tantrums, crying jags, or so-called heart attacks. These people are dictators who try to enslave you and make you do their bidding. Be firm but kind, and refuse to yield. *Appeasement never wins*. You are here to fulfill your ideal and to remain true to the eternal verities and spiritual values of life.

Give no one the power to deflect you from your goal, your aim in life, which is to express your hidden talents to the world, to serve humanity, and to reveal more and more of God's wisdom, truth, and beauty. Know definitely that whatever contributes to your peace, happiness, and fulfillment must, of necessity, bless all who walk the earth. The harmony of the part is the harmony of the whole, for the whole is in the part, and the part in the whole.

CHAPTER TWELVE

How Your Subconscious Mind Removes Mental Blocks

A young man asked Socrates how he could get wisdom. Socrates replied, "Come with me." He took the lad to a river, pushed the boy's head under the water, held it there until the boy was gasping for air, then relaxed and released his head. When the boy regained his composure, the teacher asked, "What did you desire most when you were under water?"

"I wanted air," said the boy.

Socrates told him, "When you want wisdom as much as you wanted air, you will receive it."

Likewise, when you possess an intense desire to overcome any block or addiction, and you reach a clear-cut decision that there is a way out, and that is the course you wish to follow, then victory and triumph are assured.

If you are an alcoholic or drug addict, begin by admitting it. Do not dodge the issue. Many people remain alcoholics because they refuse to admit it. If you have a burning desire to free yourself from any destructive habit, you are fifty-one percent healed. When you have a greater desire to give up a habit than to continue it, you will gain complete freedom.

Whatever thought you anchor the mind upon, the mind magnifies. If you engage the mind on the concept of freedom from habit and peace of mind, you generate feelings that gradually emotionalize the concept of freedom and peace. Whatever idea you emotionalize is accepted by your subconscious and brought to pass.

Use these steps to help cope with addiction:

FIRST
Get still; quiet the wheels of the mind. Enter into a sleepy, drowsy state. In this relaxed, peaceful, receptive state you are preparing for the second step.

SECOND
Take a brief phrase, which can readily be graven on the memory, and repeat it over and over as a lullaby. Use the phrase: *Sobriety and peace of mind are mine now, and I give thanks.* To prevent the mind from wandering, repeat the phrase aloud or sketch its pronunciation with

your lips and tongue as you say it mentally. This helps its entry into your subconscious. Do this for five minutes or more. You will find a deep emotional response.

THIRD

Just before going to sleep, imagine a friend or loved one in front of you. Your eyes closed, you are relaxed and at peace. The loved one or friend is subjectively present, and is saying to you, "Congratulations!" You see the smile; you hear the voice. You mentally touch the hand; it is all vivid and real. The word "congratulations" implies *complete freedom*. Hear it over and over until you get the subconscious reaction that satisfies.

CHAPTER THIRTEEN

How to Stay Young in Spirit Forever

Your subconscious never grows old. It is part of the universal mind of God, which was never born and will never die.

Patience, kindness, veracity, humility, good will, harmony, and brotherly love are eternal attributes, which never age. If you continue to generate these qualities, you will remain young in spirit.

During my many years of public life, I have studied the careers of famous people who have continued their productivity well beyond the normal span of life. Some achieved their greatness in old age. I have also met and known countless individuals of no prominence who, in their lesser sphere, belong to those hardy mortals who have proven that old age of itself does not destroy the creative powers of the mind and body.

My father learned French at sixty-five, and became an authority on it at seventy. He made a study of Gaelic when he was over sixty, and became a well-regarded teacher of the subject. He assisted my sister in a school of higher learning and continued to do so until he passed away at ninety-nine. His mind was as clear at ninety-nine as it was at twenty. Moreover, his handwriting and reasoning powers improved with age.

A Hollywood screenwriter told me that he had to write scripts that would cater to the twelve-year-old mind. This is a tragic state of affairs if the great masses of people are expected to be emotionally and spiritually mature. It means the emphasis is placed on youth in spite of how youth stands for inexperience, lack of discernment, and hasty judgment.

Old age really means the contemplation of the truths of God from the highest standpoint. Realize that you are on an endless journey, a series of important steps in the ceaseless, tireless, endless ocean of life. Then, with the Psalmist, you will say, *They shall still bring forth fruit in old age; they shall be fat and flourishing.* (Psalm 92:14)

You are a child of Infinite Life, which knows no end, a child of Eternity.

ABOUT THE AUTHORS

JOSEPH MURPHY was born in 1898 on the southern coast of Ireland. Raised in a devout Catholic family, Murphy had planned on joining the priesthood. As young man he instead relocated to America to make his career as a chemist and druggist. After running a pharmacy counter at New York's Algonquin Hotel, Murphy began studying mystical and metaphysical ideas. In the 1940s he became a popular New Thought minister and writer. Murphy wrote prolifically on the autosuggestive and mystical faculties of the human mind. He became widely known for his metaphysical classic, *The Power of Your Subconscious Mind*, which has sold millions of copies since it first appeared in 1963. Considered one of the pioneering voices of New Thought and affirmative-thinking philosophy, Murphy died in Laguna Hills, California, in 1981.

MITCH HOROWITZ, who abridged and introduced this volume, is the PEN Award-winning author of books including *Occult America* and *The Miracle Club: How Thoughts Become Reality*. *The Washington Post* says

Mitch "treats esoteric ideas and movements with an even-handed intellectual studiousness that is too often lost in today's raised-voice discussions." Follow him @MitchHorowitz.

ATOM-SMASHING
POWER OF MIND

ATOM-SMASHING POWER OF MIND

by Charles Fillmore

*The Life-Changing Classic
on Your Power Within*

Abridged and Introduced
by Mitch Horowitz

THE CONDENSED CLASSICS LIBRARY

Contents

Chapter Twelve
Faith Precipitations

Chapter Thirteen
The End of the Age

Charles Fillmore:
The Man Who Never Stood Still
By Mitch Horowitz

S piritual experimenters through the ages, from ancient astrologers and alchemists to contemporary chaos magicians and mind-power mystics, have always availed themselves of the latest technologies of their eras. The New Thought pioneer Charles Fillmore, who founded the vibrant and ongoing Unity movement, was a great example of this.

Born in 1854 on an Indian reservation near St. Cloud, Minnesota, Fillmore and his wife and intellectual partner Myrtle, organized their Kansas City-based Unity ministry into one of the nation's first mass-media ministries. As early as 1907, the Fillmores staffed phone banks with round-the-clock volunteers ready to assist callers with distance prayers. The Unity ministry made early use of radio, targeted mailings, correspondence courses, pamphlets, and well-produced magazines aimed at the large demographic range of Unity's congregants. This included the children's monthly *Wee Wisdom*, which launched the literary career of bestselling novelist Sidney Sheldon when it published the ten-year-old's first poem in 1927.

Up to the eve of his death in 1948, Charles Fillmore remained well versed in the science and technology of the newly dawned atomic era. Fillmore sought to unite the insights of science and practical mysticism in the collection of writings that make up *Atom-Smashing Power of the Mind*, which appeared the year after his death.

This 1949 book is one of Fillmore's finest literary efforts. It serves as a powerful and stirring summation of his theology of mind-power metaphysics. At the same time, Fillmore relates the higher abilities of thought to the revolutions in atomic energy that entered public awareness in the years immediately preceding his death. Of this, Fillmore makes a creditable effort, foreseeing future developments in wireless, microwave, and cellular technology. When I consider my failings to stay fully versed in the digital technology of our own era, I am all the more admiring of a frontier boy who grew up not only to establish a major religious denomination but who never stopped learning about the radically changing world around him. Within those changes, Fillmore discovered confirmation of his own universal ideals.

This condensation of *Atom-Smashing Power of Mind* captures the verve, spirit, and soaring language of his original, while retaining his key points and practical insights. I consider Fillmore's book one of the finest mid-century statements of New Thought philosophy. It is the kind of work that should inspire those of us today who believe that all knowledge—scientific, technological, psychological, medical, and spiritual—ultimately converge. Of this, Charles Fillmore was absolutely certain.

CHAPTER ONE

The Atomic Age

The majority of people have crude or distorted ideas about the character and the location of Spirit. They think that Spirit plays no part in mundane affairs and can be known by a person only after his death.

But Jesus said, "God is Spirit;" He also said, "The kingdom of God is within you." Science tells us that there is a universal life that animates and sustains all the forms and shapes of the universe. Science has broken into the atom and revealed it to be charged with tremendous energy that may be released and be made to give the inhabitants of the earth powers beyond expression when its law of expression is discovered.

Jesus evidently knew about this hidden energy in matter and used His knowledge to perform so-called miracles.

Our modern scientists say that a single drop of water contains enough latent energy to blow up a ten-story building. This energy, existence of which has been discovered by modern scientists, is the same kind of spiritual energy that was known to Elijah, Elisha, and Jesus, and used by them to perform miracles.

By the power of his thought Elijah penetrated the atoms and precipitated an abundance of rain. By the same law he increased the widow's oil and meal. This was not a miracle—that is, it was not a divine intervention supplanting natural law—but the exploitation of a law not ordinarily understood. Jesus used the same dynamic power of thought to break the bonds of the atoms composing the few loaves and fishes of a little lad's lunch—and five thousand people were fed.

Science is discovering the miracle-working dynamics of religion, but science has not yet comprehended the dynamic directive power of man's thought. All so-called miracle workers claim that they do not of themselves produce the marvelous results; that they are only the instruments of a superior entity. It is written in I Kings, "The jar of meal wasted not, neither did the cruse of oil fail, according to the word of Jehovah, which he spake by Elijah." Jesus called Jehovah Father. He said, "The works that I do in my Father's name, these bear witness of me."

Jesus did not claim to have the exclusive supernatural power that is usually credited to Him. He had explored the ether energy, which He called the "kingdom of the heavens;" His understanding was beyond that of the average man, but He knew that other men could do what He did if they would only try. He encouraged His followers to take Him as a center of faith and use the power of thought and word. "He that believeth on me, the works that I do shall he do also; and greater works than these shall he do."

Have faith in the power of your mind to penetrate and release the energy that is pent up in the atoms of your body, and you will be astounded at the response. Paralyzed functions anywhere in the body can be restored to action by one's speaking to the spiritual intelligence and life within them. Jesus raised His dead bodies in this way, and Paul says that we can raise our body in the same manner if we have the same spiritual contact.

What have thought concentration and discovery of the dynamic character of the atom to do with prayer? They have everything to do with prayer, because prayer is the opening of communication between the mind of man and the mind of God. Prayer is the exercise of faith in the presence and power of the unseen God. Supplication, faith, meditation, silence, concentration, are mental attitudes that enter into and form part of prayer. When one understands the spiritual character of God and adjusts himself mentally to the omnipresent God-Mind, he has begun to pray rightly.

Audible prayers are often answered but the most potent are silently uttered in the secret recesses of the soul. Jesus warned against wordy prayers—prayer uttered to be heard of men. He told His disciples not to be like those who pray on the housetop. "When thou prayest, enter into thine inner chamber, and having shut thy door, pray to thy Father who is in secret, and thy Father who seeth in secret shall recompense thee."

The times are ripe for great changes in our estimate of the abiding place and the character of God. The six-day creation of the universe (including man) described in Genesis is a symbolic story of the work of the higher realms of mind under divine law. It is the privilege of everyone to use his mind abilities in the superrealms, and thereby carry out the prayer formula of Jesus: "Seek ye first his kingdom, and his righteousness; and all these things shall be added unto you."

Of all the comments on or discussions of the indescribable power of the invisible force released by the atomic bomb none that we have seen mentions its spiritual or mental character. All commentators have written about it as a force external to man to be controlled by mechanical means, with no hint that it is the primal life that animates and interrelates man's mind and body.

The next great achievement of science will be the understanding of the mental and spiritual abilities latent in man through which to develop and release these tremendous electrons, protons, and neutrons secreted in the trillions of cells in the physical organism.

Here is involved the secret, as Paul says, "hid for ages and generations . . . which is Christ [superman] in you, the hope of glory." It is through release of these hidden life forces in his organism that man is to achieve immortal life, and in no other way. When we finally understand the facts of life and rid our minds of the delusion that we shall find immortal life after we die, then we shall seek more diligently to awaken the spiritual man within us and strengthen and build up the spiritual domain of our being until, like Jesus, we shall be able to control the atomic energy in our bodies and perform so-called miracles.

The fact is that all life is based upon the interaction between the various electrical units of the universe. Science tells us about these activities in terms of matter and no one understands them, because they are spiritual entities and their realities can only be understood and used wisely by the spiritually developed man. Electricians do not know what electricity is, although they use it constantly. The Christian uses faith and gets marvelous results, the electrician uses electricity and also gets marvelous results, and neither of them knows the real nature of the agent he uses so freely.

The man who called electricity faith doubtless thought that he was making a striking comparison when in fact he was telling a truth, that faith is of the mind and it is the match that starts the fire in the electrons and protons of innate Spirit forces. Faith has its degrees of voltage; the faith of the child and the faith of the most powerful spiritual adept are far apart in their intensity and results. When the trillions of cells in one's body are roused to expectancy by spiritual faith, a positive spiritual contact results and marvelous transformations take place.

Sir James Jeans, the eminent British scientist, gives a prophecy of this in one of his books. He says in substance that it may be that the gods determining our fate are our own minds working on our brain cells and through them on the world about us.

This will eventually be found to be true, and the discovery of the law of release of the electronic vitality wrapped up in matter will be the greatest revelation of all time.

When we awake to the fact that every breath we draw is releasing this all-potent electronic energy and it is shaping our lives for good or ill, according to our faith, then we shall begin to search for the law that will guide us aright in the use of power.

Chapter Two

The Restorative Power of the Spirit

Not only our Bible but the scriptures of all the nations of the world testify to the existence of an invisible force moving men and nature in their various activities. Not all agree as to the character of this omnipresent force, universal Spirit, but it serves the purpose of being their god under whatever name it may appear. Different nations ostensibly believe in the same scriptures, but they have various concepts of the universal Spirit; some conceive it to be nature and others God. Robert Browning says, "What I call God . . . fools call Nature."

Our Bible plainly teaches that God implanted in man His perfect image and likeness, with executive ability to carry out all the creative plans of the Great Architect. When man arrives at a certain point in spiritual understanding it is his office to cooperate with the God principle in creation.

As the animating life of all things God is a unit, but as the mind that drives this life He is diverse. Every man is king in his own mental domain, and his subjects are his thoughts.

People in this atomic-age civilization ask why God does not reveal Himself now as He did in Bible days. The fact is that God is talking to people everywhere, but they do not understand the message and brush it aside as an idle dream. We need to divest ourselves of the thought that Daniel and Joseph, in fact all the unusually wise men of the Bible, were especially inspired by God, that they were divinely appointed by the Lord to do His work. Everything points to their spiritual insight as the result of work on their part to that end.

The body is the instrument of the mind, and the mind looks to the Spirit for its inspiration. Not only the Scriptures that we look to for authority in our daily living but also the experience of ourselves and our neighbors proves that those who cultivate communion with the Father within become conscious of a guiding light, call it what you will.

Those who scoff at this and say that it is all the work of the imagination are deluding themselves and ignoring a source of instruction and progress that they need above all things. If this sense world were the only world we shall ever know, the attainment of its ambitions might be sufficient for a man of meager outlook and small capacity, but the majority of us see ourselves and the world about us in a process of transformation that will culminate in conditions here on the earth far superior to those we have imagined for heaven.

Jesus was very advanced, and His radiant body was developed in larger degree than that of anyone in our race, but we all have this body, and its development is in proportion to our spiritual culture. In Jesus this body of light glowed "as he was praying." Jesus' body did not go down to corruption, but He, by the intensity of His spiritual devotion, restored every cell to its innate state of atomic light and power. When John was in the state of spiritual devotion Jesus appeared to him, "and his eyes were as a flame of fire; and his feet like unto burnished brass." Jesus lives today in that body of glorified electricity in a kingdom that interpenetrates the earth and its environment. He called it the kingdom of the heavens.

We do not have to look to the many experiences recorded in the Bible of the spiritually illumined to prove the existence of the spiritual supersubstance. People everywhere are discovering it, as they always have in every age and clime.

The metaphysical literature of our day is very rich with the experiences of those who have found through various channels the existence of the radiant body. This prompts me to tell of my development of the radiant body, during half a century's experience. It began when I was mentally affirming statements of Truth. Just between my eyes, but above, I felt a "thrill" that lasted a few moments, then passed away. I found I could repeat this experience with affirmations. As time went on I could set up this "thrill" at other points in my body and finally it became a continuous current throughout my nervous system. I called it "the Spirit" and found that it was connected with a universal life force whose source was the Christ. As taught in the Bible, we have through wrong thinking and living lost contact with the parent life. Jesus Christ incarnated in the flesh and thereby introduced us by His Word into the original Father life. He said, "If a man keep my word, he shall never taste of death." I have believed that and affirmed His words until they have become organized in my body. Sometimes when I make this claim of Christ life in the body I am asked if I expect to live always in this flesh. My answer is that I realize that the flesh is being broken down every day and its cells transformed into energy and life, and a new body is being formed of a very superior quality. That new body in Christ will be my future habitation.

I have found that the kingdom of God is within man and that we are wasting our time and defeating the work of the Spirit if we look for it anywhere else.

CHAPTER THREE

Spiritual Obedience

Zeal is the great universal force that impels man to spring forward in a field of endeavor and accomplish the seemingly miraculous. It is the inward fire that urges man onward, regardless of the intellectual mind of caution and conversation.

Zeal should be tempered with wisdom. It is possible to be so zealously active on the intellectual plane that one's vitality is consumed and there is nothing left for spiritual growth. "Take time to be holy." Never neglect your soul. To grow spiritually you should exercise your zeal in spiritual ways.

Above all other Bible writers Paul emphasizes the importance of the mind in the transformation of character and body. In this respect he struck a note in religion that had been mute up to this time; that is, that spirit and mind are akin and that man is related to God through his thought. Paul sounds again and again in various forms this silent but very essential chord in the unity of God and man and man and his body.

When the scientific world investigates the so-called miracles of religion and discovers that they are being duplicated continually, the power of mind over matter will be heralded as of great importance to both religion and science.

Prayer gives spiritual poise to the ego, and it brings forth eternal life when spiritually linked with the Christ. "If a man keep my word, he shall never see death."

To one who gains even a meager quickening of the Spirit, Christianity ceases to be a theory; it becomes a demonstrable science of the mind.

We must not anticipate better social and economic conditions until we have better men and women to institute and sustain those conditions.

Jesus said that He was the bread and substance that came down from heaven. When will our civilization begin to realize and appropriate this mighty ocean of substance and life?

A finer civilization than now exists has been conceived by many from Plato in his "Republic" to Edward Bellamy in "Looking Backward." But a new and higher civilization will be developed only through the efforts of higher and finer types of men and women. Philosophers and seers have looked forward to a time when this earth would produce superior men and women, but save Jesus none has had the spiritual insight to declare, "Verily I say unto you, This generation shall not pass away, until all these things be accomplished."

"Behold, the man!" Jesus Christ is the type of a new race now forming in the earth. Those who incorporate into consciousness the Christ principles are its members.

The dominion that God gave to man in the beginning, as recorded in Genesis, is a dominion over spiritual ideas, which are represented in the allegory by material symbols.

Hence to exercise his dominion man must understand the metaphysical side of everything in existence.

Divine Mind is the one and only reality. When we incorporate the ideas that form Divine Mind into our mind and persevere in those ideas, a mighty strength wells up within us. Then we have a foundation for the spiritual body, the body not made with hands, eternal in the heavens. When the spiritual body is established in consciousness, its strength and power is transmitted to the visible body and to all the things that we touch in the world about us.

In the economy of the future man will not be a slave to money. Humanity's daily needs will be met in ways not now thought practical.

In the new economy we shall serve for the joy of serving, and prosperity will flow to us and through us in rippling streams of plenty. The supply and support that love and zeal set in motion are not yet largely used by man, but those who have tested this method are loud in their praise of its efficiency.

Chapter Four

I AM or Superconciousness

Superconciousness is the goal toward which humanity is working. Regardless of appearances there is an upward trend continually active throughout all creation. The superconsciousness is the realm of divine ideas. Its character is impersonal. It therefore has no personal ambitions; knows no condemnation; but is always pure, innocent, loving, and obedient to the call of God.

The superconsciousness has been perceived by the spiritually wise in every age, but they have not known how to externalize it and make it an abiding state of consciousness. Jesus accomplished this, and His method is worthy of our adoption, because as far as we know, it is the only method that has been successful. It is set forth in the New Testament, and whoever adopts the life of purity and love and power there exemplified in the experiences of Jesus of Nazareth will in due course attain the place that He attained.

Jesus acknowledged Himself to be the Son of God. Living in the superconsciousness calls for nothing less on our part than a definite recognition of ourselves as sons of God right here and now, regardless of appearances to the contrary. We know that we are sons of God; then why not acknowledge it and proceed to take possession of our God heirdom? That is what Jesus did in the face of the most adverse conditions. Conditions today are not so inertly material as they were in Jesus' time. People now know more about themselves and their relation to God. They are familiar with thought processes and how an idea held in mind will manifest itself in the body and in affairs; hence they take up this problem of spiritual realization under vastly more favorable conditions. An idea must work out just as surely as a mathematical problem, because it is under immutable law. The factors are all in our possession, and the method was demonstrated in one striking instance and is before us. By following the method of Jesus and doing day-by-day work that comes to us, we shall surely put on Christ as fully and completely as did Jesus of Nazareth.

The method by which Jesus evolved from sense consciousness to God consciousness was, first, the recognition of the spiritual selfhood and a constant affirmation of its supremacy and power. Jesus loved to make the highest statements: "I and the Father are one." "All authority hath been given unto me in heaven and on earth." He made these statements, so we know that at the time He was fully aware of their reality. Secondly, by the power of His word He penetrated deeper into omnipresence and tapped the deepest resources of His mind, whereby He released the light, life, and substance of Spirit, which enabled Him to get the realization that wholly united His consciousness with the Father Mind.

In the light of modern science the miracles of the Bible can be rationally explained as Mind acting in an omnipresent spiritual field, which is open to all men who develop spiritually. "Ye who have followed me, in the regeneration when the Son of man shall sit on the throne of his glory, ye also shall sit upon twelve thrones, judging the twelve tribes of Israel."

"He that overcometh, I will give to him to sit down with me in my throne."

Overcoming is a change of mind from error to Truth. The way of overcoming is first to place one's self by faith in the realization of Sonship, and second, to demonstrate it in every thought and act.

The Word is man's I AM. The Holy Spirit is the "outpouring" or activity of the living Word. The work of the Holy Spirit is the executive power of Father (mind) and Son (idea), carrying out the creative plan. It is through the help of the Holy Spirit that man overcomes. The Holy Spirit reveals, helps, and directs in this overcoming. "The Spirit searcheth all things, yea, the deep things of God." It finally leads man into the light.

Science rightly understood is of inestimable value to religion, and Christianity in order to become the world power that its founder envisioned, must stress the unfoldment of the spiritual mind in man in order that he may do the mighty works promised by Jesus.

When Jesus went up into the mount to pray He was transfigured before His apostles

Peter, James, and John. True prayer brings about an exalted radiation of energy, and when it is accompanied by faith, judgment, and love, the word of Truth bursts forth in a stream of light that, when held in mind, illumines, uplifts, and glorifies.

Jesus recognized Mind in everything and called it "Father." He knew that there is a faith center in each atom of so-called matter and that faith in man can move upon the faith center in so-called matter and can remove mountains.

Jesus taught that the realities of God are capable of expression here in this world and that man within himself has God capacity and power. Jesus was crucified because He claimed to be the Son of God. Yet the

Scriptures, which the Pharisees worshiped, had this bold proclamation, which Jesus quoted to them from Psalms 82:

> "I said, Ye are gods,
> And all of you sons of the Most High."

The reports by His followers of what He taught clearly point to two subjects that He loved to discourse upon. The first was the Son of God: He was the Son of God. Secondly: We might all become as He was and demonstrate our dominion by following Him in the regeneration.

In order to follow Jesus in the regeneration we must become better acquainted with the various phases of mind and how they function in and through the body.

In spiritual understanding we know that all the forces in the body are directed by thought and that they work in a constructive or a destructive way, according to the character of the thought. Medicine, massage, and all the material means accomplish but incomplete, unsatisfactory, temporary results, because they work only from the outside and do not touch the inner springs that control the forces. The springs can only be touched by thought. There must be a unity between the mind of man and Divine Mind so that ideas and thoughts that work constructively unto eternal life may be quickened in the mind and organism of man.

We are told in John that the world could not contain the books that would be written if all the things that Jesus did were put into writing. But enough is given in the story of His life and in the writings of the apostles concerning Him to bear witness to that which is daily being revealed in this day of fulfillment. Those who are consecrated to Truth and fully resolved to follow Jesus all the way are spiritualizing the whole man, including the body, which is being redeemed from corruption. Those who are living as Jesus lived are becoming like Him. "God is not the God of the dead, but of the living." Resurrection takes place in people who are alive.

CHAPTER FIVE

The Day of Judgment

It is said we are to be judged after death according to deeds done in the body, which are kept on record like books that are balanced; and if the balance is found to be in our favor we go up, and if against us we go down. But if we are spiritual now—divine—this spiritual part has dominion, and we begin to exercise this dominion. The moment we catch sight of this we begin to judge. We begin to put the thoughts that are good on the right and the others on the left. All our ideas of the attributes of our divine self we put on the right hand of power, while the thoughts of disease, death, limitation and lack we put on the left—denied, cut off.

This is not to occur after death. It is to begin right now!

Now is the time to plant the seed thought of the conditions we desire by saying, "Come my good thoughts, let us inherit our kingdom."

We do not fear anything, for we have separated our sheep from our goats; we have set our true thoughts on the right and have denied our error thoughts any power whatever.

Come into the kingdom of mind. Here everything that is in Principle is yours.

Everything, all good, is to be gathered up, and everything is good at its center. The essence of your body is good and of true substance. When you sift your consciousness of all but the real and true, the body becomes full of light.

The diamond owes its brilliance to the perfect arrangement of the innumerable little prisms within it, each of which refracts the light of the other. Man's body is made up of centers of consciousness—of light—and if arranged so they radiate the light within you, you will shine like the diamond. All things are in the consciousness and you have to learn to separate the erroneous from the true, darkness from light. The I AM must separate the sheep from the goats. This sifting begins right now and goes on until the perfect child of God is manifest and you are fully rounded out in all your Godlike attributes.

Chapter Six

Thou Shalt Decree a Thing

To decree with assurance is to establish and fix an ideal in substance. The force behind the decree is invisible, like a promise to be fulfilled at a future time; but it binds with its invisible chains the one who makes it. We have only a slight conception of the strength of the intangible. We compare and measure strength by some strong element in nature. We say "strong as steel." But a very little thought will convince us that mental affirmations are far stronger than the strongest visible thing in the world. The reason for this is that visible things lack livingness. They are not linked with energy and intelligence as are words. Words charged with power and intelligence increase with use, while material things decrease.

It is not necessary to call the attention of metaphysicians to the fact that all visible things had their origin in the invisible. The visible is what remains of an idea that has gradually lost its energy. Scientists say that this so-called solid earth under our feet was once radiant substance. Nothing is really "solid" but the atomic energy latent in everything. They tell us that it takes some six billion years for uranium to disintegrate and become lead, and this rate of disintegration has helped scientists determine the age of the earth as about two billion years.

Since nothing is lost in the many transformations that occur in nature, what becomes of the energy that is being released in the disintegration that is going on in our earth? The answer is that a new earth is being formed in which matter will be replaced by atomic energy. This process of refining matter into radiant substance is taking place not only in the natural world but in our bodies also. In fact the speed with which the transformation takes place depends on the character of the thoughts that we project into our brains and through them into our bodies and the world about us. This is why we should spiritualize our thoughts and refine the food we eat to correspond.

At the present writing there is a housing shortage everywhere and the lack of materials and competent labor indicate that several years will elapse before the need is met. This is counted a calamity; but is it? The inventive genius of man is planning houses of glass and other materials that will be much less expensive—more durable and in every respect superior to the present homes. When man gets his ingenious mind into action he always meets every emergency with something better. Every adverse situation can be used as a spur to urge one to greater exertion and the ultimate attainment of some ideal that has lain dormant in the subconsciousness.

CHAPTER SEVEN

Thinking in the Fourth Dimension

Scientists tell us that the discoveries that their efforts are revealing convince them that they are just on the verge of stupendous truths. Christianity spiritually interpreted shows that Jesus understood the deeper things of God's universe. He understood exactly what the conditions were on the invisible side of life, which is termed in His teaching the "kingdom of God" or the "kingdom of the heavens." We are trying to connect His teaching with modern science in order to show the parallel; but as He said in Mark 4:23, "if any man hath ears to hear, let him hear." This means that we must develop a capacity for understanding in terms of the atomic structure of the universe.

Unless we have this spiritual capacity we do not understand. We think we have ears, but they are attuned to materiality. They do not get the radiations from the supermind, the Christ Mind. Physiology working with psychology is demonstrating that hearing and seeing can be developed in every cell in the body, independent of ears and eyes. We hear and see with our minds working through our bodies. This being true, the capacity to hear may extend beyond the physical ear into the spiritual ethers, and we should be able to hear the voice of God. This extension of hearing is what Jesus taught. "If any man hath ears to hear, let him hear."

Then we are told that we must "take heed" what we hear. Many of us have found that as we develop this inner, spiritual hearing, we hear voices sometimes that do not tell the truth. These deceptive voices can be hushed by affirming the presence and power of the Lord Jesus Christ.

As you unfold your spiritual nature, you will find that it has the same capacity for receiving vibrations of sound as your outer, physical ear has. You do not give attention to all that you hear in the external; you discriminate as you listen. So in the development of this inner, spiritual ear take heed what you hear: discriminate.

Jesus said, "For he that hath, to him shall be given: and he that hath not, from him shall be taken away even that which he hath." How can what a man has not be taken away? We believe in our mortal consciousness that we have attained a great deal, but if we have not this inner, spiritual consciousness of reality our possessions are impermanent. Then we must be careful what we accumulate in our consciousness, because "he that hath, to him shall be given." The more spiritual Truth you pile up in your mind, the more you have of reality, and the larger is your capacity for the unlimited; but if you have nothing of a spiritual character, what little you have of intellectual attainment will eventually be taken away from you.

The mysteries of the supermind have always been considered the property of certain schools of occultists and mystics who were cautious about giving their truths to the masses for fear that in their ignorance these might misuse them. But now the doors are thrown wide open, and whosoever will may enter in.

Our attention in this day is being largely called to the revolution that is taking place in the economic world, but a revolution of even greater worth is taking place in the mental and spiritual worlds. A large and growing school of metaphysicians has made its advent in this generation, and it is radically changing the public mind toward religion. In other words, we are developing spiritual understanding, and this means that religion and its sources in tradition and in man are being inquired into and its principles applied in the development of a new cosmic mind for the whole human family.

Chapter Eight

Is This God's World?

Why doesn't God do something about it?" This oft-repeated query, uttered by the skeptical and unbelieving, is heard day in and day out. Imitating the skeptics, Christian believers everywhere are looking to God for all kinds of reforms in every department of manifest life and also are charging Him with death and destruction the world over.

One who thinks logically and according to sound reason wonders at the contradictions set up by these various queries and desires.

Is God responsible for all that occurs on this earth, and if not all, how much of it?

The Bible states that God created the earth and all its creatures, and last of all man, to whom He gave dominion over everything. Observation and experience prove that man is gaining dominion over nature wherever he applies himself to that end. But so much remains to be gained, and he is so small physically that man counts himself a pygmy instead of the mental giant that he is.

All the real mastery that man attains in the world has its roots in his mind, and when he opens up the mental realm in his being there are no unattainables. If the conquests of the air achieved in the last quarter century had been prophesied, the prophets would have been pronounced crazy. The fact is that no one thinking in the old mind realm can have any conception of the transformation of sound waves into electromagnetic waves and back again into words and messages of intelligence. Edison admitted that his discovery of the phonograph was an accident and that he never fully understood how mechanical vibrations could be recorded and be reproduced in all forms of intelligent communication.

Now that man has broken away from his limited visualizations and mentally grasped the unhampered ideas of the supermind, he is growing grandly bold and his technical pioneers are telling him that the achievements of yesterday are as nothing compared to those of tomorrow. For example, an article by Harland Manchester condensed in the *Reader's Digest* from *Scientific American* tells of the "microwaves" that are slated for a more spectacular career in the realm of the unbelievable than anything that has preceded them. This article describes in detail some of the marvels that will evolve out of the utilization of microwaves, among which may be mentioned "private phone calls by the hundreds of thousands sent simultaneously over the same wave band without wires, poles or cables. Towns where each citizen has his own radio frequency, over which he can get voice, music, and television, and call any phone in the country by dialing. Complete abolition of static and interference from electrical devices and from other stations. A hundred times as much 'space on the air' as we now have in the commercial radio band. A high-definition and color television network to cover the country. And, perhaps most important of all, a nationwide radar network, geared to television, to regulate all air traffic and furnish instantaneous visual weather reports to airfields throughout the land."

Add to this the marvels promised by the appliers of atomic energy and you have an array of miracles unequaled in all the bibles of all the nations of the world.

It is admitted by those who are most familiar with the dynamic power of these newly discovered forces that we do not yet know how to protect our body cells from the destructiveness of their vibrations. Very thick concrete walls are required to protect those who experiment with atomic forces. One scientist says that the forces released from the bombs that were used on the Japanese cities in 1945 may affect those who were subjected to them and their descendants for a thousand years. Experimentation proves that we have tapped a kingdom that we do not know how to handle safely.

CHAPTER NINE

Truth Radiates Light

Spiritual light transcends in glory all the laws of matter and intellect. Even Moses could not enter the Tabernacle when it was aglow with this transcendent light.

It is written that the Israelites did not go forward on days when the cloud remained over the Tabernacle, but when the cloud was taken up they went forward. This means that there is no soul progress for man when his body is under the shadow of a "clouded" mind, but when the cloud is removed there is an upward and forward movement of the whole consciousness (all the people).

We are warned of the effect of thoughts that are against or opposed to the commandments of Jehovah. When we murmur and complain we cloud our minds, and Divine Mind cannot reach us or help us. Then we usually loaf until something turns up that causes us to think on happier things, when we go forward again.

Instead of giving up to circumstances and outer events we should remember that we are all very close to a kingdom of mind that would make us always happy and successful if we would cultivate it and make it and its laws a vital part of our life. "The joy of Jehovah is your strength."

You ask, "How can I feel the joy of Jehovah when I am poor, or sick, or unhappy?"

Jesus said, "Come unto me, all ye that labor and are heavy laden, and I will give you rest."

Here is the first step in getting out of the mental cloud that obscures the light of Spirit. Take the promises of Jesus as literally and spiritually true. Right in the midst of the most desperate situation one can proclaim the presence and power of Christ, and that is the first mental move in dissolving the darkness. You cannot think of Jesus without a feeling of freedom and light. Jesus taught freedom from mortality and proclaimed His glory so persistently that He energized our thought atmosphere into light.

The Scriptures state that when Moses came down from Mount Sinai with the Ten Commandments his face shone so brilliantly that the Children of Israel and even Aaron, his own brother, were afraid to come near him until he put a veil over his face. The original Hebrew says his face sent forth beams or horns of light.

The Vulgate says that Moses had "a horned face;" which Michelangelo took literally, in his statue of Moses representing him with a pair of horns projecting from the head. Thus we see the ludicrous effect of reading the Bible according to the letter.

Our men of science have experimented with the brain in action, and they tell us that it is true that we radiate beams when we think. The force of these beams has been measured.

Here we have further confirmation of the many statements in the Bible that have been taken as ridiculous and unbelievable or as miracles.

Persons who spend much time in prayer and meditate a great deal on spiritual things develop the same type of face that Moses is said to have had. We say of them that their faces fairly shine when they talk about God and His love. John saw Jesus on the island of Patmos, and he says, "His countenance was as the sun shineth in his strength."

I have witnessed this radiance in the faces of Truth teachers hundreds of times. I well remember one class lesson during which the teacher became so eloquent that beams of light shot forth from her head and tongues of fire flashed through the room, very like those which were witnessed when the followers of Jesus were gathered in Jerusalem.

We now know that fervent words expressed in prayer and song and eloquent proclamations of spiritual Truth release the millions of electrons in our brain cells and through them blend like chords of mental music with the Mind universal.

This tendency on our part to analyze and scientifically dissect the many supposed miracles recorded in the Bible is often regarded as sacrilegious, or at least as making commonplaces of some of the very spectacular incidents recorded in Scripture.

In every age preceding this the priesthood has labored under the delusion that the common people could not understand the real meaning of life and that they should therefore be kept in ignorance of its inner sources; also that the masses could not be trusted with sacred truths, that imparting such truths to them was like casting pearls before swine.

But now science is delving into hidden things, and it is found that they all arise in and are sustained by universal principles that are open to all men who seek to know and apply them.

Anyone who will search for the science in religion and the religion in science will find that they harmonize and prove each other. The point of unity is the Spirit-mind common to both. So long as religion assumes that the Spirit that creates and sustains man and the universe can be cajoled and by prayer or some other appeal can be induced to change its laws, it cannot hope to be recognized by those who know that unchangeable law rules everywhere and in everything.

Again, so long as science ignores the principle of intelligence in the evolutionary and directive forces of man and the universe, just so long will it fail to understand religion and the power of thought in the changes that are constantly taking place in the world, visible and invisible.

CHAPTER TEN

The Only Mind

I say, "An idea comes to me." Where did it come from? It must have had a source of like character with its own. Ideas are not visible to the eye, they are not heard by the ear, nor felt, nor tasted, yet we talk about them as having existence. We recognize that they live, move, and have being in the realm that we term mind.

This realm of mind is accepted by everybody as in some way connected with the things that appear, but because it is not describable in terms of length, breadth, and thickness, it is usually passed over as something too vague for consideration.

But those who take up the study of this thing called mind find that it can be analyzed and its laws and modes of operation understood.

To be ignorant of mind and its laws is to be a child playing with fire, or a man manipulating powerful chemicals without knowing their relation to one another. This is universally true; and all who are not learning about mind are in like danger, because all are dealing with the great cause from which spring forth all the conditions that appear in the lives of all men and women. Mind is the one reservoir from which we draw all that we make up into our world, and it is through the laws of mind that we form our lives. Hence nothing is as important as a knowledge of mind, its inherencies, and the mode of their expression.

The belief that mind cannot be understood is fallacious. Man is the expression of mind, dwells in mind, and can know more clearly and definitely about the mind than the things that appear in the phenomenal world.

Mind is the great storehouse of good from which man draws all his supplies. If you manifest life, you are confident that it had a source. If you show forth intelligence you know that somewhere in the economy of Being there is a fount of intelligence. So you may go over the elements that go to make up your being and you will find that they draw their sustenance from an invisible and, to your limited understanding, incomprehensible source.

This source we term Mind, because it is as such that our comprehension is best related to it. Names are arbitrary, and we should not stop to note differences that are merely technical. We want to get at the substance which they represent.

So if we call this invisible source Mind it is because it is of like character with the thing within our consciousness that we call our mind. Mind is manyfold in its manifestations. It produces all that appears. Not that the character of all that appears is to be laid to the volition of Mind; no, but some of its factors enter into everything that appears. This is why it is so important to know about Mind, and how its potentialities are made manifest.

And this is where we have set up a study that makes of every atom in the universe a living center of wisdom as well as life and substance.

We claim that on its plane of comprehension man may ask the atom or the mountain the secret that it holds and it will be revealed to him. This is the communication of mind with Mind; hence we call Mind the universal underlying cause of existence and study it from that basis.

God is Mind, and man made in the image and likeness of God is Mind, because there is but one Mind, and that is the Mind of God. The person in sense consciousness thinks he has a mind of his own and that he creates thought from its own inherent substance. This is a suppositional mind that passes away when the one and only real Mind is revealed. This one and only Mind of God that we study is the only creator. It is that which originates all that is permanent; hence it is the source of all reality. Its creations are of a character hard for the sense man to comprehend, because his consciousness is cast in a mold of space and time. These are changeable and transient, while the creations of the one Mind are substantial and lasting. But it is man's privilege to understand the creations of the one Mind, for it is through them that he makes his world. The creations of the one Mind are ideas. The ideas of God are potential forces waiting to be set in motion through proper formative vehicles. The thinking faculty in man is such a vehicle, and it is through this that the visible universe has existence. Man does not "create" anything if by this term is meant the producing of something from nothing; but he does make the formless up into form; or rather it is through his conscious cooperation that the one Mind forms its universe.

Mind is the storehouse of ideas. Man draws all his ideas from this omnipresent storehouse. The ideas of God, heaven, hell, devils, angels, and all things have their clue in Mind. But their form in the consciousness depends entirely upon the plane from which man draws his mental images. If he gets a "clue" to the character of God and then proceeds to clothe this clue idea with images from without, he makes God a mortal. If he looks within for the clothing of his clue idea he knows God to be the omnipresent Spirit of existence.

So it is of the utmost importance that we know how we have produced this state of existence which we call life; and we should be swift to conform to the only method calculated to bring harmony and success into our life, namely to think in harmony with the understanding derived from communion with the God-Mind.

Chapter Eleven

The Body

You see at once that man is not body, but that the body is the declaration of man, the substantial expression of his mind. We see so many different types of men that we are bound to admit that the body is merely the individual's specific interpretation of himself, whatever it may be. Man is an unknown quantity; we see merely the various ideas of man expressed in terms of body, but not man himself. The identification of man is determined by the individual himself, and he expresses his conception of man in his body.

Some persons have tall bodies; some have short ones. Some have fat bodies; some have slim ones. Some have distorted bodies, some have symmetrical ones. Now, if the body is the man, as claimed by sense consciousness, which of these many bodies is man?

The Bible declares that man is made in the "image" and after the "likeness" of God. Which of the various bodies just enumerated is the image and likeness of God?

Let us repeat that the body of man is the visible record of his thoughts. It is the individual's interpretation of his identity, and each individual shows in his body just what his views of man are. The body is the corporeal record of the mind of its owner, and there is no limit to its infinite differentiation. The individual may become any type of being that he elects to be. Man selects the mental model and the body images it. So the body is the image and likeness of the individual's idea of man. We may embody any conception of life or being that we can conceive. The body is the exact reproduction of the thoughts of its occupant. As a man thinks in his mind so is his body.

You can be an Adam if you choose, or you can be a Christ or any other type of being that you see fit to ideate. The choice lies with you. The body merely executes the mandates of the mind. The mind dictates the model according to which the body shall be manifested. Therefore as man "thinketh within himself [in his vital nature], so is he." Each individual is just what he believes he is.

It is safe to say that nine hundred and ninety-nine persons out of every thousand believe that the resurrection of the body has something specifically to do with the getting of a new body after death; so we find more than ninety-nine per cent of the world's population waiting for death to get something new in the way of a body. This belief is not based on the principles of Truth, for there is no ready-made-body factory in the universe, and thus none will get the body that he expects. Waiting for death in order to get a new body is the folly of ignorance. The thing to do is to improve the bodies that we now have; it can be done, and those who would follow Jesus in the regeneration must do it.

The "resurrection" of the body has nothing whatever to do with death, except that we may resurrect ourselves from every dead condition into which sense ignorance has plunged us. To be resurrected means to get out of the place that you are in and to get into another place. Resurrection is a rising into new vigor, new prosperity; a restoration to some higher state. It is absurd to suppose that it applies only to the resuscitation of a dead body.

It is the privilege of the individual to express any type of body that he sees fit to ideate. Man may become a Christ in mind and in body by incorporating into his every thought the ideas given to the world by Jesus.

Divine mind has placed in the mind of everyone an image of the perfect-man body. The imaging process in the mind may well be illustrated by the picture that is made by light on the photographic plate, which must be "developed" before it becomes visible. Or man's invisible body may be compared to the blueprint of a building that the architect delivers to the builder. Man is a builder of flesh and blood. Jesus was a carpenter. Also He was indeed the master mason. He restored the Lord's body ("the temple of Jehovah") in His mind and heart (in Jerusalem).

The resurrection of the body is not dependent for its demonstration on time, evolution, or any of the man-made means of growth. It is the result of the elevation of the spiritually emancipated mind of the individual.

Step by step, thought added to thought, spiritual emotion added to spiritual emotion—eventually the transformation is complete. It does not come in a day, but every high impulse, every pure thought, every upward desire adds to the exaltation and gradual personification of the divine in man and to the transformation of the human. The "old man" is constantly brought into subjection, and his deeds forever put off, as the "new man" appears arrayed in the vestments of divine consciousness.

How to accomplish the resurrection of the body has been the great stumbling block of man. The resurrection has been a mere hope, and we have endeavored to reconcile a dying body with a living God, but have not succeeded. No amount of Christian submission or stoical philosophy will take away the sting of death. But over him who is risen in Christ "death no more hath dominion."

Chapter Twelve

Faith Precipitations

When asked what electricity is, a scientist replied that he had often thought of it as an adjunct to faith, judging from the way it acts. This linking of faith and electricity seems at first glance fantastic, but when we observe what takes place when certain substances in solution and an electric current are brought in conjunction, there seems to be a confirmation of the Scripture passage: "Now faith is assurance of things hoped for."

Just as the electric current precipitates certain metals in solution in acid, so faith stirs into action the electrons of man's brain; and acting concurrently with the spiritual ethers, these electrons hasten nature and produce quickly what ordinarily requires months of seed-time and harvest.

Speedy answers to prayer have always been experienced and always will be when the right relations are established between the mind of the one who prays and the spiritual realm, which is like an electrical field. The power to perform what seems to be miracles has been relegated to some God-selected one; but now we are inquiring into the law, since God is no respecter of persons, and we find that the fulfillment of the law rests with man or a group of men, when they quicken by faith the spiritual forces latent within them.

The reason why some prayers are not answered is lack of proper adjustment of the mind of the one who prays to the omnipresent creative spiritual life.

Jesus was the most successful demonstrator of prayer of whom we have any record, and He urged persistence in prayer. If at first you don't succeed, try, try again. Like Lincoln, Jesus loved to tell stories to illustrate His point, and He emphasized the value of persistence in prayer. He told of a woman who demanded justice of a certain judge and importuned him until in sheer desperation he granted her request.

Every Christian healer has had experiences where persistent prayer saved his patient. If he had merely said one prayer, as if giving a prescription for the Lord to fill, he would have fallen far short of demonstrating the law. Elijah prayed persistently until the little cloud appeared or, as we should say, he had a "realization;" then the manifestation followed.

Chapter Thirteen

The End of the Age

I n all ages and among all people, there have been legends of prophets and saviors and predictions of their coming.

The fact that all who believe in the principle of divine incarnation have long strained their eyes across the shining sands in an effort to catch sight of the coming of one clothed with the power of heaven, should make us pause and consider the cause of such universality of opinion among peoples widely separated. To dismiss the subject as a religious superstition is not in harmony with unprejudiced reason. To regard these prophecies merely as religious superstitions rules out traditions that are as tenable and as reliable as the facts of history. There is a cause for every effect, and the cause underlying this almost unanimous expectation of a messiah must have some of the omnipresence of a universal law.

In considering a subject like this, which demonstrates itself largely on metaphysical lines, it is necessary to look beyond the material plane to the realm of causes.

The material universe is but the shadow of the spiritual universe. The pulsations of the spiritual forces impinge upon and sway men, nations, and planets, according to laws whose sweep in space and time is so stupendous as to be beyond the ken or comprehension of astronomy. But the fact should not be overlooked that higher astronomy had its votaries in the past. The Magi and the illumined sages of Chaldea and Egypt had astronomical knowledge of universal scope. It was so broad, so gigantic, so far removed from the comprehension of the common mind of their day that it always remained the property of the few. It was communicated in symbols, because of the poverty of language to express its supermundane truths. In the sacred literature of the Hindus are evidences of astronomical erudition covering such vast periods of time that modern philosophers cannot or do not give them credence, and they are relegated to the domain of speculation rather than of science. However the astronomers of the present age have forged along on material lines until now they are beginning to impinge upon the hidden wisdom of the mighty savants of the past.

There is evidence that proves that the ages of the distant past knew a higher astronomy than do we of this age, and that they predicted the future of this planet through cycles and aeons—its nights of mental darkness and the dawn of its spiritual day—with the same accuracy that our astronomers do its present-day planetary revolutions.

Jesus evidently understood the aeons or ages through which earth passes. For example, in Matthew 13:39, our English Bible reads: "The enemy that sowed them is the devil: and the harvest is the end of the world; and the reapers are angels." In the Diaglott version, which gives the original Greek and a word-for-word translation, this reads: "THAT ENEMY who SOWED them is the ADVERSARY; the HARVEST is the End of the Age; and the REAPERS are Messengers." In this as in many other passages where Jesus used the word "age," it has been translated "world," leading the reader to believe that Jesus taught that this planet was to be destroyed.

So we see that the almost universally accepted teaching of the end of the world is not properly founded on the Bible. The translators wanted to give the wicked a great scare, so they put "the end of the world" into Jesus' mouth in several instances where He plainly said "the end of the age."

The Bible is a textbook of absolute Truth; but its teachings are veiled in symbol and understood only by the illumined.

In accordance with the prophecies of the ancients, our planetary system has just completed a journey of 2,169 years, in which there has been wonderful material progress without its spiritual counterpart. But old conditions have passed away and a new era has dawned. A great change is taking place in the mentality of the race, and this change is evidenced in literature, science, and religion. There is a breaking away from old creeds and old doctrines, and there is a tendency to form centers along lines of scientific spiritual thought. The literature of the first half of the twentieth century is so saturated with occultism as to be an object of censure by conservatives, who denounce it as a "lapse into the superstition of the past." Notwithstanding the protests of the conservatives, on every hand are evidences of spiritual freedom; it crops out in so many ways that an enumeration would cover the whole field of life.

It is evident that Jesus and His predecessors had knowledge of coming events on lines of such absolute accuracy as to place it in the realm of truth ascertained, that is, exact science.

Do you belong to the old, or are you building anew from within and keeping time with the progress of the age? The "harvest" or "consummation of the age" pointed out by Jesus is not far off. This is no theological scare; it is a statement based on a law that is now being tested and proved.

Listen to your inner voice; cultivate the good, the pure, the God within you. Do not let your false beliefs keep you in the darkness of error until you go out like a dying ember. The divine spark is within you. Fan it into flame by right thinking, right living, and right doing, and you will find the "new Jerusalem."

ABOUT THE AUTHORS

One of the pioneering leaders of the New Thought movement, CHARLES FILLMORE (1884–1948), with his with Myrtle, founded the worldwide Unity ministry. An early visionary in using mass media to spread religious and inspirational messages, Fillmore was widely known for his metaphysical interpretations of the Bible, and for his books including *Prosperity; Christian Healing; Talks on Truth; Atom-Smashing Power of Mind*; and *The Twelve Powers*.

MITCH HOROWITZ is the PEN Award-winning author of books including *Occult America* and *The Miracle Club*. A writer-in-residence at the New York Public Library and lecturer-in-residence at the University of Philosophical Research in Los Angeles, Mitch introduces and edits G&D Media's line of Condensed Classics and is the author of the Napoleon Hill Success Course series, including *The Miracle of a Definite Chief Aim* and *The Power of the Master Mind*. Visit him at MitchHorowitz.com.

THE SECRET
OF THE AGES

THE
SECRET
OF THE AGES

by Robert Collier

The Legendary Success Formula

Abridged and Introduced
by Mitch Horowitz

THE CONDENSED CLASSICS LIBRARY™

Contents

What Is the "Secret of the Ages"?

R obert Collier was born to a prosperous Irish immigrant household in St. Louis, Missouri, in 1885. As the nephew of publishing magnate P.F. Collier, the boy was part of a socially prominent family—but his early life was marked by tragedy. Robert's parents often lived apart and his mother died when he was eleven. He spent much of the remainder of his youth in boarding schools.

As Collier neared adulthood, however, he discovered a world of possibilities. He trained for the priesthood and, deciding it wasn't for him, tried his hand as a mining engineer, journalist, advertising man, and publisher.

Collier's prospects dimmed in the early 1920s when he suffered a chronic and debilitating case of food poisoning. For months the illness sapped his energies and resisted treatment. Searching for a cure, Collier dedicated himself to the study of Christian Science, prayer healing, autosuggestion, and New Thought, a popular metaphysical movement based on principle that *thoughts are causative*. Robust mental imaging, went the New Thought gospel, could restore health.

Using his new psycho-spiritual methods, Collier recovered. He came to wonder: Could the same mind-power metaphysics work for other needs, such as money and career success? Collier threw himself into studying the higher dimensions of the mind. The writer came to believe that as God had created man in His own image, so could man, through his powers of mental imaging, function as a creator within his earthly sphere of existence.

In 1926 Collier mapped out his program in a pamphlet series called *The Secret of the Ages*. He had actually begun publishing his series the prior year when, perhaps thinking of his miracle recovery, he called it *The Book of Life*.

Collier's "Secret of the Ages" was this: From earliest time, humanity has possessed the ability to invent, build, and advance through the creative energies of thought. Man's mental power, Collier explained, is a metaphysical *force* that lifted humankind out of caves and into the light of fire; it created the ancient civilizations of Egypt, Mesopotamia, and the Indus Valley; it built the empires of Greece and Rome; and its powers are encrypted in the ancient narratives, parabolic or otherwise, of every miracle from Aladdin's Lamp to Christ's walking on water.

Collier could be startlingly blunt about his views. "Mind is God," he wrote in 1927. "And the subconscious in us is our part of Divinity." But he was never cavalier. Collier expressed deep reverence for the teachings of Christ, which he considered a psychological blueprint to man's highest potential.

The metaphysical insights that aided Collier's recovery did not render him impervious to disease. He died of intestinal cancer in 1950, two years after revising and expanding *The Secret of the Ages*. But the facts of his and our physical limits should not engender cynicism toward Collier's work. His writing sparkles with sincerity and discovery, which is preserved in this condensation of his key principles. His ideas have contributed to the success of a wide range of readers, many of whom wrote to Collier during his lifetime, and have continued to make *The Secret of the Ages* a cornerstone of self-development literature in the decades since his passing.

—Mitch Horowitz

CHAPTER ONE

The World's Greatest Discovery

What, in your opinion, is the most significant discovery of our age? The finding of dinosaur eggs on the plains of Mongolia laid some 100,000,000 years ago? The unearthing of ancient tombs and cities with their specimens of bygone civilizations? The radioactive time clock by which we can estimate the age of earth at 4.5 billion years?

No—none of these. The really significant thing about this vast research from the study of bygone ages is that for the first time we are beginning to understand the existence of a "Vital Force" that—somehow, some way—was brought to earth millions of years ago.

It matters not whether you believe that mankind dates back to the primitive ape-man or sprang full-grown from the mind of the Creator. In either event, there had to be a First Cause—a source of Creation. Some Power had to bring to earth the first germ of Life.

No one can follow history down through the ages without realizing that the whole purpose of existence is GROWTH. Life is dynamic. It is ever moving forward. The one unpardonable sin of nature is to stand still, to stagnate.

Egypt and Persia, Greece and Rome, all the great empires of antiquity perished *when they ceased to grow.*

It is for men and women who refuse to stand still that this book is written. It will give you a clear understanding of your own potential, and show you how to work with and take advantage of the creative energy that surrounds you.

The evidence of this energy is everywhere. Take up some rigorous exercise—rowing, tennis, swimming, riding. In the beginning your muscles are weak, easily tired. But keep at it for a few days. The Vital Force flows into them more strongly, strengthens them, toughens them. Do rough manual labor—and what happens? The skin of your hands becomes tender, blisters, hurts. Keep it up and the Vital Force provides extra thickness, extra toughness—calluses, we call them—to meet your need.

All through daily life you will find this Life Force steadily at work. Embrace it, work with it, take it to yourself, and there is nothing you cannot do.

The fact that you have obstacles to overcome is in your favor. For when there is nothing to be done, when things run along too smoothly, this Life Force seems to sleep. It is when you need it, when you call upon it urgently, when you seem to have used up every reserve in you, that it is most on the job.

The Life Force makes no distinction between rich and poor, high and low. The greater your need, the more readily will it respond to your call. Wherever there is an unusual task, wherever there is poverty, hardship, sickness, or despair, *there* is this Servant of your Mind, ready and eager to help, asking only that you call upon it.

Chapter Two

Your Higher Self

The power to be what you want, to get what you desire, to accomplish whatever you are striving for, abides within you. It rests with you only to bring it forth. You must learn how to do that, of course, but the first essential is to *realize that you possess this power.*

You are not a mere clod. You are not a beast of burden relegated to spend your days in unremitting labor in return for food and housing. You are one of the Lords of the Earth, with unlimited potentialities. Within you is a power that, properly grasped and directed, can lead you out of mediocrity and place you among the elect— the lawgivers, the writers, the engineers, the great industrialists—the DOERS and the THINKERS. It rests with you to learn to use this Universal Mind that can do all things.

Carl Jung claimed that the subconscious contains not only all the knowledge that it has gathered during the life of the individual, but that it also contains all the wisdom of past ages. And that by drawing on its wisdom and power the individual may possess any good and noble thing of life.

You see, the subconscious is the connecting link between the Creator and ourselves, between Vital Force and our own bodies and affairs.

Most of us think of mind as merely the conscious part of us. But the earliest Greek religious writings taught that man is a triune being: *first*, the physical or conscious self; *second*, the subconscious, sometimes called your "Inner Mind" because it is latent within you; and *third*, the superconscious or "Higher Self."

Go back 2,000 years before Christ to the Upanishads, the earliest religious books of India, and you find a similar teaching. Study the religion of the Egyptians and you find the same belief. The great pyramids were triangular on each side, exemplifying the idea you find on many of their monuments. The Egyptians believed that the "Ka," or "Higher Self" could separate itself from the body and perform any service required of it.

You can send your Higher Self to do your will. Through it, you can protect your loved ones, you can heal, you can help in all ways.

To do so, however, you must charge the situation with your own Vital Force. You can never help another without giving something of yourself. You must consciously GIVE of your Vital Force. You must have the faith to SEE your Higher Self doing the things that you direct it to do. You must BELIEVE that it IS doing them. Given such faith, all things are possible to you.

YOU are a Creator, with the God-given power to use that Vital Force as you please. But to create *anything of good* requires four things:

1. The mental image of what you want. That is the mold.

2. Knowledge of your power, so you can consciously draw to you all the Vital Force you need—breathe it in—and then pour it into your mental mold.

3. Faith in your creative power, faith to crystalize the Vital Force into your mold, until it is manifest for all to see.

4. Doing something to convince your subconscious mind—and, through it, the superconscious—that you *believe you HAVE received.* For instance, a woman who prayed for a house got a board and nail and kept them before her, affirming that they were the beginning of the house.

As I see it, the Universal Mind is the Supreme Intelligence and Creator of the Universe, and we are partakers of the Divine Attributes. You are part of it, I am part of it, and anything we do *that is for the good of all* has the support of this Universal Mind—*provided we call upon it.*

Chapter Three

The Primal Cause

"Give me a base of support," said Archimedes, "and with a lever I will move the world."

Your base of support is *mind*. All started with mind. In the beginning was nothing—a fire mist. Before anything could come out of it there had to be an *idea,* a model upon which to build. *Universal Mind* supplied that idea. Therefore the primal cause is mind. Everything must start with an idea.

Matter in the ultimate is but a product of thought. Even the most materialist scientists acknowledge that matter is not as it appears. According to physics, matter, be it the human body or a log of wood, is an aggregation of distinct minute particles or atoms.

Until fairly recently, these atoms were supposed to be the ultimate makeup of matter. We ourselves—and all the material world—were supposed to consist of these infinitesimal particles, so small that they could not be seen, weighed, or touched individually—but, still, particles of matter *and indestructible.*

Now, however, these atoms have been further analyzed; and physics tells us that they are not indestructible at all—that they are mere positive and negative buttons of force or energy called protons and electrons, without hardness, without density, without solidity, without even positive actuality. In short, they are vortices in the ether—whirling bits of energy—dynamic, never static, pulsating with life.

And that, mind you, is what the solid table in front of you is made of, is what your house, your body, and the whole world is made of—*whirling bits of energy!*

Your body is about 85 percent water, 15 percent ash, phosphorus, and other elements. And they, in turn, can be dissipated into gas and vapor. Where do we go from there?

Is not the answer that, to a great degree at least, and perhaps altogether, this world is *one of our mind's own creating*?

Reduced to the ultimate—to the atom or to the electron—everything in this world is an idea of mind. All of it has been brought together through mind.

The world without is but a reflection of the world within. Your thought *creates* the conditions that the mind images. Keep before your mind's eye the image of all you want to be, and you will see it reflected in the world without.

Few of us have any idea of our mental powers. The *old idea* was that man must take this world as he found it. The basis of all democracies is that man is *not* bound by any system, that he need not accept the world as he finds it. He can remake the world to his own ideas.

As French psychologist Charles Baudouin puts it, "You will go in the direction in which you face…"

This new principle is responsible for all our inventions, all our progress. Man is satisfied with nothing. He is constantly remaking his world.

But there *must be an idea* before it can take form. As psychologist Terry Walter says: "The impressions that enter the subconscious form indelible pictures, which are never forgotten, and whose power can change the body, mind, manner, and morals; can, in fact, revolutionize a personality."

Learn to control your thoughts. Learn to image upon your mind only the things you want to see reflected there. Your thoughts supply you with limitless energy that will take whatever form your mind demands.

Begin at once, today, to use what you have learned. All growth comes from practice. All the forces of life are active—peace—joy—power.

You are "heir of God and coheir with Christ." And as such, no evil has power over you, whereas you have all power for good. And "good" means not merely holiness. Good means happiness—the happiness of everyday people.

Chapter Four

This One Thing I Do

It may sound paradoxical, but few people really know what they want.

Most of them struggle along in a vague sort of way, hoping for something to turn up. They are so occupied with the struggle that they have forgotten—if they ever knew—what they are struggling *for*. They are like a drowning man, using up many times the energy it would take to get somewhere, frittering it away in aimless struggles—without thought or direction.

You must know what you want before you stand any chance of getting it.

How did the Salvation Army get so much favorable publicity out of the First World War? They were a comparatively small part of the "services" that catered to the boys, yet they carried off the lion's share of the glory. Do you know how they did it?

By concentrating on just one thing—DOUGH-NUTS!

They served doughnuts to the boys—and they did it *well*. And that is the basis of all success in business and in most parts of life: to focus on one thing and do that thing well. Better by far to do one thing preeminently well than to dabble in forty.

The greatest success rule I know in business—the one that should be printed over everyone's desk is—"This One Thing I Do."

Volumes have been written about personal efficiency. But boiled down, it all comes to six steps:

1. Know what you want.
2. Analyze the thing you must do to get it.
3. Plan your work ahead.
4. Do one thing at a time.
5. Finish that one thing and send it on its way before starting the next.
6. Once started, KEEP GOING!

In the realm of mind, the realm of all practical power, you can possess what you want at once. You have but to claim it, visualize it, and believe in it to bring it into actuality. And all you need to begin this process is an earnest, intense, well-focused DESIRE.

"But," you will say, "I have plenty of desires. I've always wanted to be rich. How do you account for difference between my wealth, position, and power and that of the rich men all around me?"

The problem is simply that you have never focused your desires into *one great dominating desire*. You have a host of mild desires. You mildly wish you were rich, you wish you had a position of responsibility and influence, you wish you could travel at will. The wishes are so many and so varied that they conflict with each other and you get nowhere in particular. You lack one *intense* desire, to which you are willing to subordinate everything else.

Take one idea, make a good distinct picture of it, and immediately your thoughts begin to group themselves, and you have the nucleus of your desire. *This one thing you do*, and ideas from the SELF within begin to collect around the one thing, and you open the way for your good to flow to you.

Watch your thoughts! Examine each thought that comes to you. It may be your calling. Open your mind, be alert to the things happening around you. Be interested in everyone you meet; you may entertain an angel unawares. He may have a vital message for you, or you for him. Watch for your special work, recognize it, be ready for it. And when it arrives equip yourself to excel in it through study, application, and arduous practice. And, above all, *focus your efforts on this one thing.*

Do you know how Napoleon so frequently won battles in the face of a numerically superior foe? By concentrating his men at the actual *point of contact!* His artillery was often greatly outnumbered, but it accomplished far more than the enemy's because instead of scattering his fire, he *concentrated it all on the point of attack!*

The time you spend aimlessly dreaming and wishing would accomplish marvels if it were concentrated upon one definite object.

If you want a thing badly enough you will have no trouble concentrating on it. Your thoughts will naturally center on it, like bees on honey.

In his ESP experiments at Duke University, Dr. J.B. Rhine demonstrated that the mind can definitely influence inanimate objects, but only when there is intense interest or desire. When the subject's interest was distracted, when he failed to concentrate his attention, he had no power over the object. It was only as he gave his entire attention to it, concentrated his every energy upon it, that he got successful results.

Dr. Rhine proved through physical experiments what most of us have always believed: that there *is* a Power over and above the merely physical powers of the mind or body; that through intense concentration we can line up with that Power; and that once we do, nothing is impossible to us.

Chapter Five

Universal Mind

It is not always the man who struggles hardest who wins. It is the direction as well as the energy of the struggle that counts.

To get ahead you must swim with the tide. Those who prosper and succeed work in accord with natural forces. A given amount of effort with these forces carries a man faster and farther than much more effort used *against the current*. Those who work blindly, regardless of these forces, make life difficult for themselves and rarely prosper.

It has been estimated that something like 60 percent of the factors producing success or failure lie outside of a man's conscious efforts—separate from his daily round of details. To the extent that he cooperates with the wisdom and power of Universal Mind he is successful, well, and happy. To the extent that he fails to cooperate, he is unsuccessful, sick, and miserable.

The connecting link between your conscious mind and Universal Mind is *thought*. And every thought that is in harmony with progress and good, every thought that is freighted with the right idea, can penetrate to Universal Mind. And penetrating to the Universal Mind, your thought returns with the power of Universal Mind to accomplish it. You don't need to originate the ways and means. The Universal Mind knows how to bring about any necessary results.

There is one right way to solve any problem. When your human judgment is unable to decide what that one right way is, turn to Universal Mind for guidance. You need never fear the outcome; if you heed its advice you cannot go astray.

A flash of genius does not originate in your own brain. Through intense concentration you establish a circuit through your subconscious mind with the Universal, and it is from the Higher Mind that the inspiration comes. All genius, all progress comes from this same source.

Chapter Six

See Yourself Doing It

What does it mean that *God created man in His own image*?

"The imagination," writes Glenn Clark in *The Soul's Sincere Desire*, "is of all the qualities in man the most Godlike—that which associates him most closely with God. The first mention we read of man in the Bible is where he is spoken of as an 'image.' 'Let us make man in our own image, after our likeness.' The only place where an image can be conceived is in the imagination."

If man was made in God's image, it stands to reason that man's imagination—like that of the Great Master—is capable of creation.

When you form a mental image of the good you wish to come to pass, make it clear, picture it vividly in every detail, BELIEVE in it, and the "Genie-of-Your-Mind" will bring it into being as an everyday reality.

The keynote of successful visualization is this: *See things as you would have them be instead of as they are.*

Close your eyes and make clear mental pictures. Make them look and act just as they would in real life. In short, daydream—but daydream with a *purpose*. Better still, get those pictures down on paper using, if you need to, pictures of similar things cut from magazines. Concentrate on one idea at a time to the exclusion of others, and continue to concentrate on that one idea until it has been accomplished.

CHAPTER SEVEN

The Formula of Success

What is the eternal question that stands up and looks you and every sincere person squarely in the eye each morning?

"How can I better my condition?" That is the real-life question that confronts you, and will haunt you every day till you solve it.

Often this question takes the form of whether you should stick to the job you have, or seek a better one. The answer depends entirely on what you are striving for. The first thing is to set your goal. What is it you want? A profession? A political career? An executive position? A business of your own?

Every position should yield you three things:

1. Reasonable pay for the present.
2. Knowledge, training, or experience that will be worth money to you in the future.

3. Prestige or acquaintances that will be of assistance
    in attaining your goal.

Judge every opening by these three standards. But
don't overlook chances for valuable training, merely because the pay is small.

Some complain of their station in life and feel that
their surroundings are discouraging. Do you feel that
if you were in another's place success would be easier?
Just bear in mind that your real environment is *within
you*. All the factors of success or failure are in your inner
world. *You* make your own inner world—and through
it your outer world. You can choose the material from
which to build. If you have chosen unwisely in the past,
you can choose new material now. The richness of life
is within you. Start right in and do all those things you
feel you have it in you to do. *Ask permission of no one.*

Take the first step and your mind will mobilize all
of its forces to your aid. But it is essential is that you
begin.

Those who have made their mark on life all had one
trait in common: they *believed in themselves*. "But," you
may ask, "how can I believe in myself when I have never
done anything worthwhile, when everything I put my
hand to seems to fail?" You can't, of course. That is,
you couldn't if you had to depend upon your conscious

mind alone. But remember what one far greater than you said: "I can of mine own self do nothing. The Father that is within me—He doeth the works."

That same "Father" is within you. And it is by knowing that He *is* in you, and that through Him you can do anything that is right, that you can acquire the belief in yourself that is so necessary.

The starting point is *Faith*. But St. James tells us: "Faith without works is dead." So go on to the next step. Decide the one thing you want most from life. No matter what it may be. There is no limit to Mind. Visualize this thing that you want. See it, feel it, BELIEVE in it. Make your mental blueprint, and *begin to build!*

Psychologists have discovered that the best time to make suggestions to your subconscious is just before going to sleep, when the senses are quiet and the body is relaxed. So, let us take your desire and suggest it to your subconscious mind tonight. The two prerequisites are the earnest DESIRE, and an intelligent, understanding BELIEF.

Do that every night until you ACTUALLY DO BELIEVE that you have the thing you want. When you reach that point, *YOU WILL HAVE IT!*

The Law of Attraction

Look around you. What businesses are getting ahead? Who are the big successes? Are they the ones who grab the passing dollar, careless of what they offer in return? Or are they those who are striving always to give a little greater value, a little more work than they are paid for?

When scales are balanced evenly, a trifle of extra weight thrown on either side overbalances the other as effectively as a ton.

In the same way, a little better value, a little extra effort, makes the man of business stand out from the great mass of mediocrity, and brings results out of all proportion to the additional effort involved.

It pays—not merely altruistically, but in good, hard dollars—to give a little more value than seems necessary, to work a bit harder than you are paid for. It's that extra ounce of value that counts.

For, the Law of Attraction is service. We receive in proportion as we give out. In fact, we usually receive in far greater proportion.

"Whosoever shall be great among you," said Jesus, "shall be your minister, and whosoever of you will be the chiefest, shall be the servant of all." In other words, if you would be great, you must serve. And he who serves most shall be greatest of all.

If you want to make more money, instead of seeking it for yourself see how you can make more for others. In the process you will inevitably make more for yourself, too. We get as we give. *But we must give first.*

It matters not where you start—you may be a day laborer. But still you can give—give a bit more of energy, of work, of thought, than you are paid for. Try to put a little extra skill into your work. Use your mind to find some better way of doing whatever task may be set for you.

There is no kind of work or method that cannot be improved by thought. So give generously of your thought to your work. Think every minute you are at it: "Isn't there some way this could be done easier, quicker, better?" Read everything that relates to your own work, or to the job ahead of you.

Look around YOU now. How can YOU give greater value for what you get? How can you SERVE better?

How can you make more money for your employers, or save more for your customers? Keep that thought ever in front of you and *you'll never need to worry about making more money for yourself.*

Chapter Nine

Your Needs Are Met

An old man called his children to his bedside to give them a few parting words of advice. "My children," he said, "I have had a great deal of trouble in my life—a great deal of trouble—*but most of it never happened.*"

We are all like that old man. Our troubles weigh us down, in prospect, but we usually find that when the actual need arrives, Providence has devised some way of meeting it.

In moments of great peril, in times of extremity, when the brave soul has staked its all—those are the times when miracles are wrought, if we but have faith.

That does not mean that you should rest supinely at your ease and let the Lord provide. When you have done *all that is in you to do*—when you have given your very best—don't worry or fret as to the outcome. Know that if more is needed, your need will be met. You can sit back with the confident assurance that, having done your part, you can depend upon the Genie-of-Your-Mind to do the rest.

This does not mean that you will never have difficulties. Difficulties are good for you. They are the exercise of your mind. You are the stronger for having overcome them. But look upon them as mere exercise, as "stunts" that are given you in order to better learn how to use your mind, and how to draw upon Universal Supply. Like Jacob wrestling with the Angel, don't let your difficulties go until they have blessed you—until, in other words, you have learned something from having encountered them.

CHAPTER TEN

The Master Mind

The Transcendentalist philosopher Ralph Waldo Emerson wrote: "There is one mind common to all individual men. Every man is an inlet to the same and to all of the same. He that is once admitted to the right of reason is made a freeman of the whole estate. What Plato has thought, he may think; what a saint has felt, he may feel; what at any time has befallen any man, he can understand. Who hath access to this universal mind is a party to all that is or can be done, for this is the only and sovereign agent."

The great German physicist Walther Nernst found that the longer an electric current was made to flow through a filament, the greater became the conductivity of the filament.

In the same way, the more you call upon and use your subconscious mind, the greater becomes its conductivity in passing along to you the infinite resources of Universal Mind. The wisdom of a Solomon, the skill of Michelangelo, the genius of an Edison, the daring of a Napoleon, *all* may be yours. It rests with you only to form contact with Universal Mind in order to draw from it what you will.

Think of this power as something that you can connect with at any time. It has the answer to all of your problems. There is no reason why you should hesitate to aspire to any position, any honor, any goal, for the Mind within you is fully able to meet any need. It is no more difficult for it to handle a great problem than a small one. Mind is just as much present in your everyday affairs as in those of a big business or a great nation.

Start something! Use your initiative. Give your mind something to work upon. The greatest of all success secrets is *initiative*. It is the one quality, more than any other, that has put men in high places.

Conceive something. Conceive it first in your own mind. Make the pattern there and your superconscious mind will draw upon the plastic substance or energy all about you to make that model real.

The connecting link between the human and the Divine, between the formed universe and formless energy, lies in your imaging faculty. It is, of all things human, the most God-like. It is our part of Divinity. Through it we share in the creative power of Universal

Mind. Through it we can turn the drabbest existence into a thing of life and beauty. It is the means by which we avail ourselves of all the good that the Universal Mind is constantly offering.

When Jesus adjured His disciples, "whatsoever ye desire, when ye pray, believe that ye RECEIVE it," He was not only telling them a great truth, but he was teaching what we moderns would call excellent psychology, as well. For this "belief" is what acts upon the subconscious mind and through it upon the superconscious. It is through this "belief" that formless energy is compressed into material form.

The Apostles were almost all poor, uneducated men, yet they did a work that is unequalled in history. Joan of Arc was a poor, illiterate peasant girl—yet she saved France. So don't allow lack of training, lack of education, to hold you back. Your mind can meet every need, and direct you to every necessary step.

The pages of history are filled with ordinary people who went on to think great thoughts, forge great nations, build and invent great things, and became religious, political, or commercial leaders. *Begin now.* Use the glorious empire of your mind to build that which you yearn to see in the world, that which would help yourself and others.

Use the infinite horizons of your mind—a part of the Universal Mind, a part of Divinity.

About the Authors

Born in St. Louis, Missouri, in 1885, ROBERT COLLIER trained for the priesthood before entering a career in business. He achieved success in the fields of advertising, publishing, and engineering. After struggling with a severe and chronic case of food poisoning, Collier recovered using methods of Christian Science, New Thought, prayer therapy, and autosuggestion. He made an intensive study of the new metaphysics and distilled what he learned into a popular and influential pamphlet series first called *The Book of Life* in 1925 and renamed *The Secret of the Ages* in 1926. Collier assembled *The Secret of the Ages* into a single volume, which he revised and expanded in 1948. The author of many books on the mystical dimensions of the mind, Collier died in 1950.

MITCH HOROWITZ, who abridged and introduced this volume, is the PEN Award-winning author of books including *Occult America* and *The Miracle Club: How Thoughts Become Reality*. *The Washington Post* says Mitch "treats esoteric ideas and movements with an even-handed intellectual studiousness that is too often lost in today's raised-voice discussions." Follow him @MitchHorowitz.

Printed in the USA
CPSIA information can be obtained
at www.ICGtesting.com
JSHW012031140824
68134JS00033B/2999